Abraham JT Harris, BBS

Scripture quotations identified from Holy Bible, New International Version. NIV. Copyright @ 2012 by YouVersionBibleApp. YouVersion.com

Scripture quotations identified from Holy Bible, New King James Version. NKJV. Copyright @ 2012 by YouVersionBibleApp. YouVersion.com

Scripture quotations identified from Holy Bible, Amplified. AMP. Copyright @ 2012 by YouVersionBibleApp. YouVersion.com

Scripture quotations identified from Holy Bible, English Standard Version. ESV. Copyright @ 2012 by YouVersionBibleApp. YouVersion.com

Scripture quotations identified from Holy Bible, New Living Translation. NLT. Copyright @ 2012 by YouVersionBibleApp. YouVersion.com

JOURNEY INTO HEALING
TAKE TIME TO HEAL
By
Abraham JT Harris, BBS

Abraham JT Harris, BBS

Journey Into Healing: Take Time To Heal
Abraham JT Harris, BBS

Published By Parables
April, 2021

All Rights Reserved. No part of this book may be reproduced or utilized in any form or by any means, electronic or mechanical, including photocopying, **recording, or by any information storage and retrieval system, without permission in writing from the author.**

    ISBN 978-1-945698-98-9
    Printed in the United States of America

Readers should be aware that Internet Web sites offered as citations and/or sources for further information may have been changed or disappeared between the time this was written and the time it is read.

JOURNEY INTO HEALING
TAKE TIME TO HEAL
By
ABRAHAM JT HARRIS, BBS

PUBLISHED by PARABLES
Earthly Stories with a Heavenly Meaning

Abraham JT Harris, BBS

Acknowledgement

I want to acknowledge the Holy Spirit most importantly. I am growing in a deeper relationship with the Spirit of God. I thank Him because without Him nothing is possible. I can do all things through Him and nothing without Him. He has taken me on a journey to emotional healing. I did not realize how hurt and broken I was until it all came crashing down one night. I genuinely believe as preachers of the gospel, we forget to guard our hearts and ask the Holy Spirit to search us through and through. As a result, we become silently disgruntled towards ministry and people. Ministry is not an easy calling. Therefore, we must rely on the ministry of the Holy Spirit to empower, guide, heal, and teach us. So, in saying that, I dedicate this book to the most consistent person in my life. It is the formidable Holy Spirit!

Abraham JT Harris, BBS

Dedication

I dedicate this book to my church family. I am a pastor to the most caring people. You all have caused me to be a better leader and a better man. I love and appreciate all of you. I pray for you and I want you to soar as I do. Let's allow God to take us where He desires, and remember that He wants us to cling to Him.

Introduction:

I thought it was important to write on this subject because I am all too familiar with pain and hurt. Also, as a pastor, life coach, and a Christian Counselor, I see firsthand what happens when people do not take time to heal. I think as believers of Jesus, we use the Scriptures as means not to deal with internal hurts, afflictions, and pain. In this book, I am hoping to shine light on some areas regarding emotional and mental healing. I am hoping that through reading these Scriptures, my personal experience and stories from others will help people. Then, we can begin a beautiful journey of wholeness and healing. In order to be effective in ministry, life, and with family, we must be whole and complete. It is time for our healing! Let's do this together. All the names in this book have been changed for respect of privacy.

Abraham JT Harris, BBS

Chapters:

1. What hurt?

2. Does Time really heal all wounds?

3. The Process (Forgiveness)

4. Mental Prison

5. True Brokenness

6. Pursing Healing

7. True Freedom

Study Questions

Chapter 1- What Hurt?

As we begin this journey together, we must first discover truth. It is hard to believe the truth about ourselves, and it takes candor to recognize that you are bleeding, hurting, and in pain. It is a reality we never want to face. As humans, we are great at adapting. What does it mean to adapt? It means to make (something) suitable for a new use or purpose; modify.1

When tragedy and hurt happens in our lives, we learn how to make our pain comfortable and tolerable by altering, reshaping, and modifying ourselves. This makes us into a person we were not created to be. We do not even understand why we react in certain ways. The answer is not hard to discover. You need healing!

We must acknowledge that we are hurting. We can no longer hide behind our smiles, jobs, Facebook posts, Snapchat stories, or any other entities that we entrench our lives with.

A Tale of a Runner

This story I want to tell you is about someone I think I know quite well. It is about myself. This is not easy to admit, but until I was truthful with myself, I could not truly move forward. I was one that could not deal with difficult situations, nor could I have difficult conversations. So, I would run from these things and try not to look back.

I remember being faced with a situation where my phone was being stolen at night and looked through by someone close to our family. I had personal content in my phone where I was talking a friend through a situation. If you didn't know the situation (which I will not share) you would take the conversation for something it is not intended to be.

For weeks I didn't understand why I was being treated differently. I heard whispers when I was around some people.

One day a friend told me "Hey man, your name is on ice!"

I said to him, "What does that mean?"

He replied, "You are being discussed by your friends, family and enemies. They are you saying you are trying to sleep with Tony because of some text message."

Despite Tony telling people about the situation, you know how rumors and gossip can get out of hand. After this, I started experiencing a feeling I had never felt. For the first time in my life I retreated within myself so far that I ran and hid for months. I switched to an online school, I got a job where I worked at night, and I didn't go to stores. In my spare time I couldn't stand being awake, so I took sleeping pills to sleep all day. This was the beginning of my marathon.

I learned from that situation how to run from issues, how not to feel, how to not cope with the pain, and how to silence the hurt. After all, I wasn't really hurting. I just didn't want to deal with fake people. Being by myself is what I like best anyway. As time went on, I slowly stopped running and hiding. I was finally back in full swing with many of the same people. We never talked about it again. It was like it never happened. On the surface, this is excellent, but what I didn't realize is this situation set the tone for how I would deal with emotional pain for years to come. I got good at moving on like most people. I did not know I had not truly moved forward in my life. Moving on and moving forward are two very different things.

Moving on Vs. Moving Forward

In our ability to adapt lies the problem that we never deal with the hurt that is within us. We move on but what we don't realize is everything that has happened to us "moves on" as well. Let's look at what it means to "move on" versus what it means to "move forward."

A Friend shares Her Story

I asked this question to a friend to help give you other perspectives to the path to healing.

Question:
Think of a time when you "moved on" but you carried that hurt, pain, or persons with you. How did this affect your life?

Her Story:
Winter of 2009 I decided to walk away from an unhealthy relationship. I came into that relationship with baggage from a previous one, hoping and expecting to truly be loved the right way. I thought the baggage would go away if I entered a new situation. So, there I was, damaged goods with another who was just as damaged as I was. I let my guard down again, and I opened myself up because I felt safe. Being that I never truly healed from the first relationship, I now added more wounds.

I measured my worth by a ruler with one being the lowest. I was one. The aftermath of my situation affected not only me, but the people around me as well. All I could think about was "How in the world did I get here?

I participated in intimate acts that I would never do. I suffered abuse and humiliation. It was all because I never took the time to heal from previous hurt and pain! This was so I could be strong enough to know that taking time to heal was okay, and being alone was okay too."

I now carried guilt, and I took on a broken thought that all men would be the same! He was the son of a well-known Pastor in the city, but it meant nothing. There was no way I could completely fault him. I blamed myself every day for the next few months, and I walked with shame and hurt. Why did I deserve to be cheated on when I was faithful? I went against the people I love, family, friends, God, and my own standards. I tried to hold on to what was already damaged. My life was even more shattered. Feeling worthless I knew leaving was the best thing I had done.

Move on: 1. Go in a specified direction or manner; change position. 1.6. Go quickly. 2
Move Forward: toward or at a place, point, or time in advance; onward; ahead: *to move forward; from this day forward; to look forward.* 3

There is an incredible difference in these two definitions. When you simply move on, you go to your next place or relationship, almost with the sense of running. I know from my experience that moving on seems great at first. Soon after, many things become all too familiar because I have not dealt with the internal damage. Moving forward is acknowledging what has happened, and taking the time to deal with the damage that has been done. After I have dealt with the hurt, pain, and trauma, I use those experiences to help me progress in my life. It also helps in my future relationships and opportunities.

Acknowledgement goes a long way!

I began my journey as a Pastoral-Christian Counselor a few years ago. I have always been driven with the passion to help people. I must admit that no amount of schooling, coaching, or training prepared me for what I was getting ready to face as I counseled people. School gave me great tools, but it is nothing like experiencing it. I began my journey by counseling and coaching about five clients. There was one that threw me for a loop. I started counseling a woman named Daisy, who was in her late 20's. Daisy had been through two marriages and a series of other relationships and friendships. Daisy, upon coming to me, found herself alone and without hope. She had no relationships with friends, family, or a mate.

Daisy commenced to tell me about her past marriages. She talked about the verbal abuse the two inflicted on each other. She demonized the men to the point of sickness for me. She told me she couldn't believe the men were now happily married and had children. She felt the need to reach out to the wives to expose how deplorable these men were. She couldn't believe the responses of these other women. The women told of how amazing these men were. They were loving, compassionate, and caring to them. She was astonished by this! Daisy was convinced that these women were being bamboozled. I just sat, took notes and listened further.

She eventually moved on to talk about her family. She shared about how she was out casted, ostracized, and how she felt like the black sheep of the family. Her relationships were combative and full of arguments. She talked about being invited to family gatherings and functions. Whenever she did show up an argument was bound to break out. She continued, this time with ex friends. She talked about how she was always being left out and gossiped about. She shared how a group of friends ended their friendship with her abruptly one day.

At this point my head was swimming. I had all kinds of thoughts. My immediate reactions were that she was being victimized by all these people. I thought that this woman had the world against her, and I started counseling from that angle. I started speaking to her value and worth. I started talking to her about being comfortable with who see was. As time went on, she started sharing more. A light hit me so hard as I began to pray about Daisy and her situation. Why light? Because it exposed what I was seeing and what she was not saying.

I started sensing through the Holy Spirit that something traumatic had happened to Daisy, and as a result, it was affecting her relationships and her life. I started feeling that her pain and hurt was the reason her relationships were constantly being shipwrecked.

At our third session, I brought what I was feeling to Daisy. She broke down in tears. I could feel her pain through her deep cry. She began to share about being raped by a family member for years while growing up. This experience haunted her, and the pain was crippling. The pain had been destructive to everything in her life. I was the first one she had shared this with. She acknowledged what happened to her, and as a result, this affected her relationships, career, and overall life.

The journey to healing was a long and, at times, difficult one. However, it started when she acknowledged the pain. She said after that session she felt a weight lift off once she said what she had experienced. Acknowledgement is powerful. You cannot heal what you hide. Daisy is now a mother of three and happily married with a career helping abused women. The healing all started with acknowledgement.

If Only
Jeremiah 3:13-14 AMP

Only understand fully and acknowledge your wickedness and guilt, that you have rebelled (transgressed) against the Lord your God. And have scattered your favors among strangers under every green tree, and you have not obeyed My voice,' says the Lord. 'Return, O faithless children [of the twelve tribes],' says the Lord, 'For I am a master and husband to you, And I will take you [not as a nation, but individually]—one from a city and two from a [tribal] family— And I will bring you to Zion.'

I know these verses have to do with an acknowledgement of sin, but there is still a lesson to be learned regarding this subject.

First let's explore the meaning of "Acknowledge" in this verse. The Hebrew word is "Yâda." It is a verb meaning: to know, to learn, to perceive, to discern, to experience, to confess, to consider, to know how, to be skillful, to be known, to make oneself known, to make to know.

The backdrop of this verse is that Israel had turned her back on God who has been a faithful Husband to the nation. They had served and worshipped other gods and went against God's commandments. Through the Prophet Jeremiah, God saw that Israel played the harlot with many lovers. (See: Jeremiah 3:1) He tells them that they have spoken and done evil things. (Verse 5) The Lord continues by talking about how unfaithful the nation had been. He stated he is longing for them to return to Him. The nation would face the pain they were putting themselves through. He says to them in verse 13, "Only acknowledge your sin." How powerful is that?

Acknowledgement was half the battle. If they would have acknowledged their failures to fall God's way, they more than likely would have made the necessary steps to see restoration. God wanted to bring them to a new place. What does this teach us? When we have the strength to acknowledge the ugly truth, we will want to see change. We will not want to be the same after exposing the pain that dwells within us. Restoration and wholeness are possible, but it starts with acknowledgement. You cannot keep denying what is going on within you.

A Lesson from King David
Psalm 13:1-6 **NIV**

"How long, Lord? Will you forget me forever? How long will you hide your face from me? How long must I wrestle with my thoughts and day after day have sorrow in my heart? How long will my enemy triumph over me? Look on me and answer, Lord my God. Give light to my eyes, or I will sleep in death, and my enemy will say, 'I have overcome him,' and my foes will rejoice when I fall. But I trust in your unfailing love; my heart rejoices in your salvation. I will sing the Lord's praise, for he has been good to me."

When dealing with matters of the heart, I like to look at David. My main reason for looking at King David is because of the fact that he was a man after God's own heart (1 Samuel 13:14; Acts 13:22) and he was constantly pouring out his pain, hurt, and distress to God. In Psalm 13, David starts out with several questions for God. He recognized the sorrow in his heart. I love how David admits this. David shows us that after acknowledging the sorrow, we should turn to God with trust. This is key if we are going to start to heal. We must trust the process and, most importantly, trust God.

As we take this journey together, we must first be open to acknowledging the pain, hurt, and trauma. You cannot afford to live in denial any longer. Hear these words from God speaking from His words to our heart: If you only acknowledge what you are dealing with.

Questions for Reflection:

1. Have you moved on without truly moving forward?

2. Have you been hiding your pain in the hopes that you can live with it?

3. Are you willing to acknowledge what is going on inside of you?

4. Can you identify with any story that was told in this chapter?

5. What are you hoping to gain from reading this book?

Prayer

     Father, we thank you Lord for our lives. We thank you for our experiences. God, we pray for the strength to acknowledge the pain we have learned to live with. We recognize that we are weak, but when we are weak, you are strong. We confess that we cannot take this journey in our own strength, but we can do all things through You who gives us strength. I understand that this journey will not be easy at times, but I know it is necessary, so that we can be whole and healed. Keep our hearts diligent through this process. Thank you in advance for the freedom we will experience. In Jesus Name, Amen.

Chapter 2: Does Time Really Heal all Wounds?

Psalm 6: 2-3 *NIV*
"Have mercy on me, Lord, for I am faint; heal me, Lord, for my bones are in agony. My soul is in deep anguish. How long, Lord, how long?"

I remember experiencing deep pain after my parents split up. The emotional pain was manifesting as physical pain. I remember that my chest hurt as if I was having a heart attack. I remember my head pounding as if it was about to explode. After speaking with someone about how I was feeling they told me, "You must endure this pain, it is a natural human response. Time will heal your wounds." I had heard this saying plenty of times before. I believed it because I thought about how many times growing up as an adventurous kid, I would get cuts and abrasions that would heal with time. I came to know just how wrong that statement was. A year went by, and I was just as hurt and angry as I was before. It wasn't until I started to treat the wound through prayer, conversation, and counsel that I started to feel relief.

David Fireman, LCSW writes.

"Time in itself—unlucky for us—does not heal all wounds… The passage of time may take the edge off acute pain, but it does not heal pain. On the other hand, time can be used well for healing purposes. When time is used well, in terms of healing wounds, then it is because we do something specific with and within it."6

These statements are so true. What you do with that time is what truly matters. Taking time to heal must be intentional and active. Time is the indefinite continued progress of existence and events in the past, present, and future regarded as a whole.7 Looking at this definition of time it seems, when it comes to healing, that it does nothing but prolong pain when pain is not properly dealt with.

Not worth the wait

Liz had a very painful experience. She was engaged with whom she believed to be the love of her life. After 6 months of being engaged she began to see changes in her fiancé's behavior. She started to suspect that he was being unfaithful. A few more months went by, and they were growing extremely distant. Liz decided to confront her fiancé on the matter. Liz could not even imagine what she was about to hear. Her fiancé began to tell her that he slept with her sister, but it only happened once. The distance was due to the guilt he was feeling with himself. He stated that he was in love with her and wanted a chance to right his wrong. Liz, after thinking about it, believed that in time she would heal, forgive, and trust him again. She knew that the love they had for one another would be enough to get them through.

They moved on from the situation and got married. Liz didn't realize how hard it would really be to heal and let go. After 3 months of marriage, she finally reached out for help. Liz said that every day after this happened, she played it on repeat. She did not trust him, she was disgusted when sleeping with him, and she could not imagine getting over it. She wondered why after all this time the pain hadn't gone away even a little. Liz decided to separate from her now husband and seek emotional and mental healing. It was a long process of forgiving and healing. Her husband worked on healing in his own way because he was so guilt stricken. He was also in pain. Liz and her husband are now married going on four years traveling the world.

What did they do? They took time to heal. They were intentional with the time they gave each other. They were committed to wholeness through the power of useful time. I believe "useful time" is time that is used to accomplish a task or to get a result.

A Look at Leah
Genesis 29 NIV

Then Jacob continued on his journey and came to the land of the eastern peoples. There he saw a well in the open country, with three flocks of sheep lying near it because the flocks were watered from that well. The stone over the mouth of the well was large. When all the flocks were gathered there, the shepherds would roll the stone away from the well's mouth and water the sheep. Then they would return the stone to its place over the mouth of the well.

Jacob asked the shepherds, "My brothers, where are you from?"

"We're from Harran," they replied.

He said to them, "Do you know Laban, Nahor's grandson?"

"Yes, we know him," they answered.

Then Jacob asked them, "Is he well?"

"Yes, he is," they said, "and here comes his daughter Rachel with the sheep."

"Look," he said, "the sun is still high; it is not time for the flocks to be gathered. Water the sheep and take them back to pasture."

"We can't," they replied, "until all the flocks are gathered, and the stone has been rolled away from the mouth of the well. Then we will water the sheep."

While he was still talking with them, Rachel came with her father's sheep, for she was a shepherd. When Jacob saw Rachel daughter of his uncle Laban, and Laban's sheep, he went over and rolled the stone away from the mouth of the well and watered his uncle's sheep. Then Jacob kissed Rachel and began to weep aloud. He had told Rachel that he was a relative of her father and a son of Rebekah. So, she ran and told her father.

As soon as Laban heard the news about Jacob, his sister's son, he hurried to meet him. He embraced him and kissed him and brought him to his home, and there Jacob told him all these things. Then Laban said to him, "You are my own flesh and blood."

After Jacob had stayed with him for a whole month, Laban said to him, "Just because you are a relative of mine, should you work for me for nothing? Tell me what your wages should be."

Now Laban had two daughters; the name of the older was Leah, and the name of the younger was Rachel. Leah had weak eyes, but Rachel had a lovely figure and was beautiful.

Jacob was in love with Rachel and said, "I'll work for you seven years in return for Rachel."

Laban said, "It's better that I give her to you than to some other man. Stay here with me." So, Jacob served seven years to get Rachel, but they seemed like only a few days to him because of his love for her.

Then Jacob said to Laban, "Give me my wife. My time is completed, and I want to make love to her."

So, Laban brought together all the people of the place and gave a feast. But when evening came, he took his daughter Leah and brought her to Jacob, and Jacob made love to her. And Laban gave his servant Zilpah to his daughter as her attendant. When morning came, there was Leah! So, Jacob said to Laban, "What is this you have done to me? I served you for Rachel, didn't I? Why have you deceived me?"

Laban replied, "It is not our custom here to give the younger daughter in marriage before the older one. Finish this daughter's bridal week; then we will give you the younger one also, in return for another seven years of work."

And Jacob did so. He finished the week with Leah, and then Laban gave him his daughter Rachel to be his wife. Laban gave his servant Bilhah to his daughter Rachel as her attendant. Jacob made love to Rachel also, and his love for Rachel was greater than his love for Leah. And he worked for Laban another seven years.

When the Lord saw that Leah was not loved, he enabled her to conceive, but Rachel remained childless. Leah became pregnant and gave birth to a son. She named him Reuben, for she said, "It is because the Lord has seen my misery. Surely my husband will love me now."

She conceived again, and when she gave birth to a son she said, "Because the Lord heard that I am not loved, he gave me this one too." So, she named him Simeon.

Again, she conceived, and when she gave birth to a son she said, "Now at last my husband will become attached to me, because I have borne him three sons." So, he was named Levi.

She conceived again, and when she gave birth to a son she said, "This time I will praise the Lord." So, she named him Judah. Then she stopped having children.

This story has always been intriguing to me. It says that the Lord saw that Leah was not loved so he opened her womb to conceive. It is amazing to me that God saw her heartache and pain. Not only did God see that Leah was hurting, but he responded to it by blessing her with the beautiful gift of having children. What is interesting to me is that Leah responds back, and she starts to name the children out of her broken place. Let's look at these names and their meanings.

Reuben: "It is because the Lord has seen my misery." *(Verse 32)*

Simeon: "Because the Lord heard that I am not loved, he gave me this one too." *(Verse 33)*

Levi: "Now at last my husband will become attached to me, because I have borne him three sons." *(Verse 34)*

Leah believed with time as she birthed these sons that her husband would love her that way she wanted to be loved. She thought that this would bring healing to her and the situation. After she realized that this would not be the case, she made a choice to see it differently. She had a proper response to the gifts that God had blessed her with.

Genesis 29:35

"She conceived again, and when she gave birth to a son she said, 'This time I will praise the Lord.' So, she named him Judah. Then she stopped having children."

She had to realize that though the situation would not change, she could change her perspective and ultimately be at peace within herself. It was all because God had shown her His kindness.

What have you named or spoken over out of your hurting place? I know that in my life I have done this all too often. I have been blessed with beautiful things by God, only to destroy them with my thinking and words. I responded to the gifts of God with the pain I self-sabotaged because I wanted to feel loved and accepted by people. This is a common response among people. We look at what we are not getting, so we destroy what we are receiving by the Lord. We must change our perspective, and the only way to do that is to realize that your pain has blinded you from seeing the blessings in your life.

Don't Question Me

I remember working with Rashad on several projects. When I asked him questions on what he was doing, and what his thinking behind his work was, he would get indifferent and shut down. This went on for a while. I noticed it, but I never said anything about it. We just continued to work on projects.

Suddenly, it got to the point where it started to affect our work, so I opened the conversation. I asked him "Why do you get offended at questions?"

He replied, "I don't like to be questioned. Don't question me."

I explained that my questions are to learn and to know people's way of thinking. He ended the conversation.

A couple of days went by, and I was careful about what I said especially in the form of a question. He approached me, and stated that he realized that this started when he was a kid. His parents questioned his every move and every decision. What was built in him was a sense that he could never do anything right. The pain of that was still there as if he was 14 years old again. We had several more conversations about this. Through this process, it opened the door for conversation with his parents and healing came.

Time did not heal this wound. It was the strength to confront the ugly reality that he was hurting, and it was spreading to other areas of his life.

There is A Time
Ecclesiastes 3:1-8 NIV

"There is a time for everything, and a season for every activity under the heavens: a time to be born and a time to die, a time to plant and a time to uproot, a time to kill and a time to heal, a time to tear down and a time to build, a time to weep and a time to laugh, a time to mourn and a time to dance, a time to scatter stones and a time to gather them, a time to embrace and a time to refrain from embracing, a time to search and a time to give up, a time to keep and a time to throw away, a time to tear and a time to mend, a time to be silent and a time to speak, a time to love and a time to hate, a time for war and a time for peace."

Time is an amazing thing. For many aspects in our lives, time itself doesn't change much, but working toward a task in a specific frame of time does change things. Take the time to heal. Commit to becoming whole. I speak over you in the Name of Jesus Christ: this is your appointed time to be healed.

Isaiah 41:10 NIV

"So, do not fear, for I am with you; do not be dismayed, for I am your God. I will strengthen you and help you; I will uphold you with my righteous right hand."

I want to encourage you as you walk through this journey because fear will try to grip you. The biggest obstacle will be the big question of 'what if?' 'What if I do this and nothing changes?' 'What if this makes my pain worse?' 'What if I start getting depressed?' We have been living our lives in the 'what if's' for far too long.

Now is the time to be free from every hurt and pain that is holding you captive. Feelings and emotions will flow through you like a river. It will feel like you do not have the courage to endure this journey. You will feel uncomfortable at times. Just look at what Isaiah 41:10 NIV says: "So do not fear, for I am with you; do not be dismayed, for I am your God. I will strengthen you and help you; I will uphold you with my righteous right hand."

"I will strengthen you" means He will cause you to be strong. "I will help you" means He will make your life easier to bear and He will bear it with you. "I will uphold you" means He will support and defend you. You will get through this. You will become who you were created to be: Free!

Questions for Reflection:

1. Have you ever believed that time could heal your wounds? If so, how did it work out?

2. Have you ever experienced physical pain because of a heartache? How did you deal with this? What did you learn?

3. What are some triggers that stem from past pain? What appropriate steps can you take to bring healing?

4. Can you identify with Leah? If so, in what ways? How can you change your perspective so that healing can happen?

5. Are you ready to put useful time and action together?

Prayer:
    Lord, we thank you for our time together. We thank you for the gift of time. We are asking you to help us use our time wisely. We know your word says there is a time for everything. Jesus, we believe that this is our time to be healed. Help us to no longer wait things out, hoping in time it will fix itself. We are believing You for change as we take this this journey to heal. Help us to no longer name our blessings after pain. Help us receive the blessings You have given us with praise and thanksgiving. In Jesus name, Amen.

Chapter 3- The Process (Forgiveness)

Colossians 3:13 NIV
"Bear with each other and forgive one another if any of you has a grievance against someone. Forgive as the Lord forgave you."

There is an assortment of great material and books on the subject of forgiveness. There is not much to add but I do want to share some perspectives and experiences with you.

Forgiveness is an easy concept but a hard reality. I used to pride myself on being someone who could forgive easily. I seemingly was one who would be angry with someone, but in 20 minutes I would be totally fine with the same person I was mad at before. I soon discovered that was not the reality. I was internalizing everything for an outward image. I liked the image of being someone who was not fazed by anything. This pride was deceptive, and it even deceived me into believing that I had feelings of steel. I was walking around tricked by myself.

I had perfected this behavior for years, and even as an adult, I struggled with this. What I didn't realize was that I was building unforgiveness in my heart. I was temporarily dismissing my pain only to dwell on it in my private time. It would replay it like a rerun of a television show. I would stew in my thoughts of anger and pain only to dismiss it once more as if it wasn't a problem. I would lay in bed night after night being tormented by the agonizing pain of things that were said and done to me. I was having painful dreams of the events I had been through over and over. I was suffering with the worst case of unforgiveness that I have ever heard about.

Let's explore the meaning of forgiveness in Greek.

Forgiveness: "*aphesis*" Release, as from bondage, imprisonment. A sending away, a letting go, a release, pardon, complete forgiveness. The letting them go, as if they had not been committed.

This meaning of forgiveness is astounding. I want to look closely at the words "Release, as from bondage, imprisonment." I love this because to not forgive is complete entrapment. I remember being so full of unforgiveness that when I would see the person it would change my mood immediately. That, my friends, is bondage. No person should ever have that much power over you. When you hold something against someone your emotions become bound to that person.

Forgiving Yourself

The hardest person to forgive in my life has been myself. Think about this. The biggest expectations you ever give to yourself start with this statement, "When I grow up, I am going to be…" Whether we realize it or not, that is an expectation we put on ourselves. Many people look back on that statement and are very disappointed about how their life turned out. Think about how hard you have been on yourself when failing at a task. I would resort to putting myself down verbally. This is true with most of the ignorant choices I have made in my life. I felt like the person I should be able to count on was myself. This haunted me throughout my life even with the smallest incidents. I would ask God and others to forgive me, and I had high hopes that they would. However, when it came to myself, I couldn't release it.

One day I heard this verse read in a Bible study. *Psalm 103: 8-12 NIV: The Lord is compassionate and gracious, slow to anger, abounding in love. He will not always accuse, nor will he harbor his anger forever; he does not treat us as our sins deserve or repay us according to our iniquities. For as high as the heavens are above the earth, so great is his love for those who fear him; as far as the east is from the west, so far has he removed our transgressions from us.*

Someone also read this verse. *Hebrews 8:12 NIV: For I will forgive their wickedness and will remember their sins no more.*

Then this hit me. If God is willing to remove my sin and remember it no more, then why am I dwelling on it? He should hold all my wrong against me, especially since from a young child I was taught The Way. I lived in this constant state of self-condemnation. I thought I should know better.

I prayed this simple prayer; "Lord, give me the strength and will to forgive myself." I prayed this every day. It didn't happen right away, but I started to feel relief. This was the first step in my forgiveness process. If I was not willing to forgive myself, I was definitely not able to extend forgiveness to anyone else.

A Story Shared

I asked Belinda this question, so she could help us in our Journey:

Describe a time when it was hard to forgive. What were the effects of unforgiveness? How did you get free from this bondage?

Her Response:

I had a very hard time forgiving my ex-husband. He was abusive and cheated a lot. I thought by hanging onto the unforgiveness and bitterness I was protecting myself form being hurt again. But, in reality, it caused me to distrust everyone I encountered, especially men. So instead of having fun and enjoying life, I isolated myself. The Lord moved my son and I to North Carolina to start the healing process. He said I was not created to be an island or a peninsula, meaning only partially attached, but in middle America fully surrounded by people. He then asked me to forgive my ex-husband. I got really upset and self-righteous with God. I was angry at God for even asking such a thing. Did He even know what all he did to me? How dare God ask me. He wouldn't have if He knew what had happened to me. God then told me in a very stern voice "I didn't die just for you". Then and there I let go, and forgave my ex-husband. I trusted the Father that He had something better for us. That was the beginning of my journey to complete freedom and healing.

Surrender My Right

An important part in the forgiveness process is to surrender our right to be angry, along with giving up our right to hold it against the offender. We justify not forgiving because we think we are entitled to how we feel. That may ring true for you, but anger turns into pain. Who is really suffering? If you do not let it go you will be stuck in time. It is time to come off the spin cycle and move forward.

Truth is we have no right to hold anything against someone. We are forgiven by God, so now we must extend that forgiveness. We must remember that we all need grace. We all have messed things up big time. That is what we, as humans, do. Some of the things that we hold against someone is something we have done to other people.

A Conscious Choice
Ephesians 4:32 NIV
"Be kind and compassionate to one another, forgiving each other, just as in Christ God forgave you."

The "ing" in "forgiving" is saying to me that the process is ongoing. This is letting us know that it will be a continuation. I know for me, choosing to walk in forgiveness is a choice I must make every single day. Even when I have forgiven someone, it takes an occasional reminder to myself and I have to choose to release them.

If I am being honest when I have not forgiven someone, those things show up in my thoughts and even in my dreams. Therefore, I must make a conscious choice to forgive.

The Biggest Regret
I recall a story of an older woman. Her late husband had been unfaithful for several years. She knew about the affair for the entire time it was happening. She hired a private investigator, who provided pictures to prove the unfaithfulness. She never approached her husband about it, and he died thinking this affair was a secret. This woman retreated so far within herself that she could never find the strength to forgive him. She was relieved when he died. She thought when he passed

away, she would feel better and not feel worthless. She soon found that the pain was even more agonizing with each passing day. She lived 15 years after her husband. She grew more hateful and venomous. She went to church every week and was known as mean and hateful. She distanced herself from her two boys because they were a reminder of her late husband. She didn't have any meaningful relationship during this period of her life. Then, she was hospitalized due to health complications. During this time, the pastor of the church she attended provided counseling, prayer, and support. With his help, she reconciled with her boys and forgave her late husband. She was in great standing with her children and with God. She felt so free in her final months on Earth. Forgiveness was the key to her freedom.

Matthew 18:21-35 NIV

Then Peter came to Jesus and asked, "Lord, how many times shall I forgive my brother or sister who sins against me? Up to seven times?" Jesus answered, "I tell you, not seven times, but seventy-seven times.

"Therefore, the kingdom of heaven is like a king who wanted to settle accounts with his servants. As he began the settlement, a man who owed him ten thousand bags of gold was brought to him. Since he was not able to pay, the master ordered that he and his wife and his children and all that he had be sold to repay the debt. "At this the servant fell on his knees before him. 'Be patient with me,' he begged, 'and I will pay back everything.' The servant's master took pity on him, canceled the debt and let him go. "But when that servant went out, he found one of his fellow servants who owed

him a hundred silver coins. He grabbed him and began to choke him. Pay back what you owe me!' he demanded. "His fellow servant fell to his knees and begged him, 'Be patient with me, and I will pay it back.' "But he refused. Instead, he went off and had the man thrown into prison until he could pay the debt. When the other servants saw what had happened, they were outraged and went and told their master everything that had happened. "Then the master called the servant in. 'You wicked servant,' he said, 'I canceled all that debt of yours because you begged me to. Shouldn't you have had mercy on your fellow servant just as I had on you?' In anger his master handed him over to the jailers to be tortured, until he should pay back all he owed. "This is how my heavenly Father will treat each of you unless you forgive your brother or sister from your heart."

People choose to not forgive for actions that they are known to do themselves. This man was forgiven of a huge debt, but he didn't extend that same forgiveness to someone else. This is what we do all too often. We hold people to a standard that we do not require of ourselves. This should not be. If we want grace, we need to extend grace. If we want mercy, we need to extend mercy. If we want compassion, we need to extend compassion. If we want to be forgiven, we need to forgive.

I want to share some of my favorite quotes about forgiveness:

Rick Warren Quote:
"And you know, when you've experienced grace and you feel like you've been forgiven, you're a lot more forgiving of other people. You're a lot more gracious to others."

Frederick W. Robertson Quote:
"We win by tenderness. We conquer by forgiveness"

C.S. Lewis Quote:
"To be a Christian means to forgive the inexcusable, because God has forgiven the inexcusable in you."

Henry Ward Beecher Quote:
"I can forgive, but I cannot forget, is only another way of saying, I will not forgive. Forgiveness ought to be like a cancelled note – torn in two, and burned up, so that it never can be shown against one."

Forgiveness sets us free. When you forgive you will feel lighter, and you will feel joy return to you. Make the choice to live free.

Questions for Reflection:
1. Are you holding unforgiveness in your heart?

2. Read Psalm 103: 8-12. What do these verses mean to you? What revelation did you receive?

3. Do you feel entitled to your pain? Are you willing to surrender it to God?

4. What is your biggest obstacle to forgiveness?

5. Which forgiveness quote spoke to you more and why?

Prayer:
    Father, we thank you for opening our eyes to the many things in this chapter. We pray that you help us in the area of forgiveness. We know in order to be forgiven; we must first forgive. We recognize and acknowledge that this cannot be done in our own strength. We need you to teach us the way of forgiveness, empowered by your Holy Spirit. You sent your Spirit to help us, and we need your help in this area. Help us to see our offenders as You see them. Help us to bear with one another with compassion. We pray just as King David in Psalm 51: 10 KJV did, "Create in me a clean heart and renew the right spirit within me." Give us forgiving spirits Father. We ask this in the matchless Name of Jesus. Amen.

Abraham JT Harris, BBS

Chapter 4- Mental Prison

__Psalm 142: 1-4__ NIV
"I cry aloud to the Lord; I lift up my voice to the Lord for mercy. I pour out before him my complaint; before him I tell my trouble. When my spirit grows faint within me, it is you who watch over my way. In the path where I walk people have hidden a snare for me. Look and see, there is no one at my right hand; no one is concerned for me. I have no refuge; no one cares for my life."

    I connect with this prayer so deeply from King David. David wrote this while he was in a cave. I don't know about you but a lot of times I feel as if I am in a cave, or I feel like I want to run into one. I feel so trapped within myself at times. I have felt as if my pain was too strong for me. I have been completely wrecked! This type of devastation can lead to a mental prison. I define a mental prison as being trapped in your own thoughts, feelings, and emotions with no relief. When you are in this state, it doesn't matter what others say or do. You can only view it one way. I can speak to this because I have been there many times.

    I have also been the one that needed to be seen. Until the last few years, because of my hurt and pain, I have had this issue. I thought everyone was always after me or talking bad about me. I would create a narrative in my own head that no one really wanted me to succeed. I felt like my relationships were always going to be temporary because I was not deserving of lasting relationships. This was a mental prison fueled by my pain. I would isolate to where I would be attacked with overwhelming desires that I was trying to run from. The desire to be loved and accepted. So, I would self-sabotage by engaging in text conversations that I knew should not been happening because many were very sexual in nature. Why am I sharing this? Because this was all driven by unacknowledged pain. I felt like people would talk to me on the level that they loved me. Many times I had no desire to even be with the person like that, but it was a cry for acceptance. Pain will cause you to self-sabotage. Your hurt will tell your mind what you need in order to feel better, and many times it is in unhealthy ways.

Emotions Taking Over

God created us with emotions. The key is letting emotions work for you and not letting your emotions control you. Emotions are to be kept in proper perspective. When controlled by your emotions, you become susceptible to thinking in ways that are not healthy. Emotions will allow you full freedom to make things up. Out-of-control emotions do not care about facts or reasoning. Therefore, it is very important that you fully understand that you feel and communicate those feelings appropriately. God not only created us with emotions, but He also has emotions.

God Has Compassion
Psalm 86:15 NIV

"But you, Lord, are a compassionate and gracious God, slow to anger, abounding in love and faithfulness."

God Hates Sin
Psalm 11:5 NIV
"The Lord examines the righteous, but the wicked, those who love violence, he hates with a passion."

God Gets Angry
Psalm 106:40 NIV
"Therefore, the Lord was angry with his people and abhorred his inheritance."

God Can Grieve
Ephesians 4:30 NIV
"And do not grieve the Holy Spirit of God, with whom you were sealed for the day of redemption."

God Rejoices
Isaiah 62:5 NIV
"As a young man marries a young woman, so will your Builder marry you; as a bridegroom rejoices over his bride, so will your God rejoice over you."

God Gets Jealous
Deuteronomy 4:24 NIV
"For the Lord your God is a consuming fire, a jealous God."

I believe God gave us emotions so we can experience life at its fullest. God's emotions come from a place of righteousness and justice. We must submit our emotions under His control. Emotional decisions can lead to further devastation and heartache. We must filter our emotions through truth. How can we make that happen? By praying and relying on the Spirit of Truth to lead you.

(See: John 14:17) You may think that you can't find the words to pray. God knows what we are trying to say through tears, screams, or words. We must be open to His leading, realizing that He wants the best outcome for us.

I Couldn't Get Out of My Head

I recall counseling several people that were tormented mentally by their thoughts. These thoughts were stemming from deep emotions. In all these cases, the problem was a heart issue that waged a war in their mind. They could not get past how they felt about the situations in order to make clear decisions. I have been here many times in my life as well. This is the place many people find themselves; it is a prison. I want to help you with what I have learned when dealing with your emotions, so they don't imprison you mentally. You must experience them, express them, and exit them.

Experience Emotions

Experience Meaning: the fact or state of having been affected by or gained knowledge through direct observation or participation.10

It is okay to allow yourself to feel the emotions. I find that when I try to suppress my emotions, I am not being true to my natural human experience. Through this, I can understand just how much I am affected.

Express Them

Express Meaning: to give or convey a true impression of.11

Expressing your feelings should always be done in an appropriate way through self-control. Sometimes things can be dealt right away when you express how someone made you feel or how they offended you. It is equally important to express your emotions to yourself. I do this through reflections and journaling.

Exit Them

Exit Meaning: the act of going out or away.12

This concept has to do with emotions such as anger, rage, sadness, etc. It has been too often that I have camped out in these emotions. I did not allow them to go away. I felt protected by my anger, but it just made me miserable. *Ephesians 4:26-27 NIV says "In your anger do not sin: Do not let the sun go down while you are still angry, and do not give the devil a foothold."* It is okay to experience anger, but you also must allow it to be released. Do not remain in anger. Let all these types of emotions take their exit.

Break-Out of Your Prison
Romans 12:2 NIV

"Do not conform to the pattern of this world, but be transformed by the renewing of your mind. Then you will be able to test and approve what God's will is—his good, pleasing and perfect will."

Ephesians 4:22-24 NIV

"You were taught, with regard to your former way of life, to put off your old self, which is being corrupted by its deceitful desires; to be made new in the attitude of your minds; and to put on the new self, created to be like God in true righteousness and holiness."

It is possible to start thinking differently. It is possible to break out of your mental prison, but your mind must be renewed. How we deal with hurt and pain changes when your mind is renewed.

Greek Meaning
Renewed: *Anakainoó*
Make new again; To renew by moving from one stage to a higher one.

This definition is amazing, through the renewing of our minds we move from one stage to a higher one. This means we rise above what has happened to us. It is possible for our minds to be clear and free from the pressures of pain. You can rise above it. You deserve to rise above it. You renew your mind by learning your identity in Christ through his word.

Proverbs 23:7a KJV
"For as he thinketh in his heart, so is he."

What we think we can become. You can think from a place of pain and become pain. You can think from a place of hurt and become hurt. A person in pain often causes pain. Do not let this becomes your identity. Do not be a victim to this anymore, because you can overcome it. It is time to hope and dream again. Don't let what has happened to keep you mentally bound. I will say it again; you can rise above all the hurt and pain.

Questions for Reflection:

1. Do you feel that you are in a mental prison regarding a situation?

2. Do you have control over your emotions?

3. Do you allow yourself to experience your emotions?

4. What steps can you take to escape negative emotions?

5. Are you ready for your mind to be renewed?

Prayer:

      Lord, we thank You for the gifts You have given us. We thank You for emotions that we can experience and enjoy. We pray for You to help us submit our emotions under Your control through the Holy Spirit. Father, help us break out of our mental prison through the renewal of our minds. In the name of Jesus Christ, Amen.

Abraham JT Harris, BBS

Chapter 5- True Brokenness

Psalms 51:17 NKJV
"The sacrifices of God are a broken spirit, A broken and a contrite heart— These, O God, you will not despise."

I think that many believers stay in a place of being broken because they don't really know what it means. Many used being broken as an excuse to stay in a place of hurt and pain.

I asked several people to share what brokenness means to them. Below are some responses to my question.

Person 1:
Brokenness comes through life experiences. It is hard when you have been damaged before, but now you are ready to be used fully by God.

Person 2:
Brokenness is being crushed and struck down. Because of this, you are open to the things of the Spirit.

Person 3:
I believe brokenness is realizing that you can do nothing without Christ. Brokenness is humbling yourself under God's mighty hand.

Person 4:
Brokenness means to be broken from sin.

Let's explore Psalm 51 and the background story so we can understand this subject more.

When the kings were supposed to be off to war. David sent the army of Israel out with Joab. While the war was going on David stayed at his palace in Jerusalem. One evening he was on the roof, while up there he saw Bathsheba bathing, she was the wife of Uriah. David had her brought up to him and he slept with her. Later, she came back to King David and told him she was with Child. David began to plot on how he could cover it up. David brought Uriah to the palace to persuade him to go home and rest, he also sent a gift to Uriah. Long story short, Uriah did not go home to rest and sleep with his wife. David went further with plotting, he put Uriah on the front line of the battlefield to be killed. This really displeased the Lord; he sent a prophet to rebuke him. *(See: 2 Samuel 11:1-27 NIV)*

Psalms 51:1-19 NJKV

Have mercy upon me, O God, according to Your lovingkindness; According to the multitude of Your tender mercies, Blot out my transgressions. Wash me thoroughly from my iniquity and cleanse me from my sin. For I acknowledge my transgressions, and my sin is always before me. Against You, you only, have I sinned, and done this evil in Your sight— That You may be found just when You speak, and blameless when You judge. Behold, I was brought forth in iniquity, and in sin my mother conceived me. Behold, you desire truth in the inward parts, and in the hidden part You will make me to know wisdom. Purge me with hyssop, and I shall be clean; Wash me, and I shall be whiter than snow. Make me hear joy and gladness, That the bones You have broken may rejoice. Hide Your face from my sins and blot out all my iniquities. Create in me a clean heart, O God, and renew a steadfast spirit within me. Do not cast me away from Your presence, and do not take Your Holy Spirit from me. Restore to me the joy of Your salvation and uphold me by Your generous Spirit. Then I will teach transgressors Your ways, and sinners shall be converted to You. Deliver me from the guilt of bloodshed, O God, The God of my salvation, and my tongue shall sing aloud of Your righteousness. O Lord open my lips, and my mouth shall show forth Your praise. For You do not desire sacrifice, or else I would give it; You do not delight in burnt offering. The sacrifices of God are a broken spirit, A broken and a contrite heart— These, O God, you will not despise. Do good in Your good pleasure to Zion; Build the walls of Jerusalem. Then You shall be pleased with the sacrifices of righteousness, with burnt offering and whole burnt offering; Then they shall offer bulls on Your altar.

I wanted to give you the complete story so that we can look at this together. David messed up big time. He got himself into a horrible predicament. David was anointed by God, he was a great warrior, a man full of wisdom, and a man after God's own heart (See 1 Samuel 13:14, Acts 13:22).

Sometimes when you feel as if you have been so anointed and in a great place with God, pride comes in. You feel as if you can get away with things. I believe David was in this thought pattern. Although he loved God, and was after His heart, pride is a cunning thing and can corrupt anyone. After David had done this terrible thing, God sent the prophet Nathan to confront him (See 1 Samuel 12). David responded with brokenness. Psalm 51 is David's prayer and heart's cry. He came broken before the Lord. Broken? Yes, broken from the sin and pride. We should all have this response. We miss the mark every day, but instead of making excuses for it, our response should be that of brokenness.

Brokenness definition: In the positive, spiritual sense, brokenness is the condition of being completely subdued and humbled before the Lord, and as a result, completely yielded to and dependent upon Him also. (Deep Truths, James Arendt)

Contrite definition: to break or bruise; to rub or wear... Literally, worn or bruised. Hence, broken-hearted for sin; deeply affected with grief and sorrow for having offended God; humble; penitent; as a contrite sinner.15

I am using a lot of Scripture and meaning to help you really understand about brokenness. We use broken before the Lord as an excused to not heal. We are ministering, singing, speaking, and we are bleeding. I can recall a time where there was a woman minister who was always ministering out of an angry place. She would blast people over the microphone. When she would rebuke, it would be full of venom. Although this would happen, her ministry still had signs and wonders. So she was sought after by many. She came to our ministry, and she once again ministered out of that same place. My pastor was able to kindly confront her on this, and she received his gentle rebuke. The words went into her heart. She took time to clear her schedule, and she was healed with the help of the Holy Spirit. When she came back, her ministry exploded. It was not just occasional signs and wonders, but a true display of His presence. Instead of being hurt, broken and beaten, she had been perfectly broken before the Lord. This brokenness was that of humility and total dependency on the Holy Spirit.

Psalm 34:17-20 NIV
The righteous cry out, and the Lord hears them; he delivers them from all their troubles. The Lord is close to the brokenhearted and saves those who are crushed in spirit. The righteous person may have many troubles, but the Lord delivers him from them all; he protects all his bones, not one of them will be broken.

God is near to those who are brokenhearted because He is the healer. He doesn't require us to have a broken heart to be near to us. This Scripture is telling us that we can find comfort in the fact that our God is close when we have been hurt. He saves us from a crushed spirit and delivers us from trouble. This means that we don't have to stay in the place of pain. You can experience wholeness in your life.

Matthew 5:3 NIV
"Blessed are the poor in spirit, for theirs is the kingdom of heaven.

This simply talks about those who are humble. This is the brokenness we must experience. We must acknowledge our sin, pain, and hurt and give it to our

Lord Jesus Christ. This is true brokenness, we are not called to walk around full of hurt, pain and a broken heart. We can pursue the healing that was provided for us through the Lord's sacrifice.

Questions for Reflections:

1. What is your definition of "brokenness?"

2. Which person did you agree with more? Person 1, 2, 3 or 4?

3. In what ways can you identify with King David?

4. Are you completely yielded to God? If not, why?

5. In what ways do you need to humble yourself before God?

Prayer:

　　　Father, we thank You for being near to us in whatever state we are in. Lord, we want to be truly broken before You and humbly rely on You. We want to depend on You and not our own strength. Forgive us, God, for our trespasses, just as David prayed. Create in us a clean heart, and renew a right spirit within us. We repent of every known sin; we ask You to reveal to us any unknown sin. We want to be people after Your own heart. We thank You for saving us from a crushed spirit and delivering us from our troubles. We thank You for hearing us. Let us respond to Your call with true brokenness. In Jesus Name, Amen.

Abraham JT Harris, BBS

Chapter 6: Pursing Healing
Exodus 15:26b NIV
"For I am The Lord, who heals you."

God is Jehovah-Rapha. He is the God who heals us. I do not have any special words I can say that will heal you. This book is simply a tool to help in your journey. I am only writing to provoke you to break old mindsets, confront the pain, and pursue healing that was bought and paid for through the blood of Jesus Christ. Healing belongs to every believer that will receive it. Yes, that includes emotional and mental healing. The Healer will be willing and able to heal every wound you have, no matter how long it's been there or how bad it hurts. I am not perfect, and I am healing in some areas, but I do know that I am far better off than a couple of years ago. I found the strength through Christ and realized that my broken life was not what God wanted for me. Nor did I want it for myself.

Stop Stuffing

Some people are great at stuffing their hurt. They get hurt and internalize it as if nothing is wrong. They move on as if the person did nothing. The problem is every time the person does something, and you don't release it appropriately, you allow the cut to go deeper. It is time to unpack. You've been on the "trip of pain" too long. The Bible gives us a great remedy for those who like to stuff things. Our answer is found in *Matthew 18:15-16 NIV "If your brother or sister sins, go and point out their fault, just between the two of you. If they listen to you, you have won them over. But if they will not listen, take one or two others along, so that 'every matter may be established by the testimony of two or three witnesses."* You will be amazed what a conversation will do. This is not to say you will not feel pain or hurt, but you can stop it from spreading and going deeper by releasing it through conversation.

Healing Belongs to Us

Stacy, who is a mother of three, shared her story with me. She is a domestic violence victim. She was abused by her ex-husband for many years. Stacy told me that being beaten emotionally and mentally was worse than being beaten physically. After years of this, she finally found the strength to leave him. The only problem was with her next few relationships, she attracted the same type of men. Although she was never physically abused again, the men were very verbally abusive. After seeking help, she soon discovered that because she was shattered and didn't take the necessary time to heal her pain, she thought these men were attractive. She ended those relationships, and got help so she could heal. Stacy is now ministering to women who have been abused physically, emotionally, and mentally. Although Stacy is not yet remarried, she says, "I understand my worth in Christ."

Your Pain Will Attract More Pain

What is interesting about Stacy's story is that her pain attracted the same type of men as her ex-husband who caused pain. I know in my own life, the very thing that caused me pain I allowed to come back in a different form. When you are not pursing healing, it is hard to break the cycle. You will only see through the eyes of hurt and pain. We have human tendencies to go back to what is familiar to us even if it hurts us. This is no way to live. There is better for us. Healing will allow you to know that you are worth more than what you are putting up with and allowing.

Meaning of Healing

I want to look at some different meanings of healing.

1. Heal, Healing [Verb] *iaomai* "to heal," "made whole."

2. Heal, Healing [Verb] *sozo* "to save," is translated by the verb "to heal"

3. Heal, Healing [Noun] *iasis* akin to *iaomai*, stresses the process as reaching completion.

4. Heal, Healing [Verb] *therapeuo* primarily signifies "to serve as a *therapon*, and attendant.

Healing: the process of making or becoming sound or healthy again. (Dictionary.com)

Healing: to cause (an undesirable condition) to be overcome: MEND. to patch up or correct (a breach or division). (Merriam- Webster)

Healing: the process in which a bad situation or painful emotion ends or improves. (Cambridge Dictionary)

These definitions gave me a good sense of what healing really means. When we become emotionally, mentally, and even physically damaged, there is a breach that takes place. Another way I could put it is there is a tear that takes place. You do not feel complete or whole, and you feel as if you are not yourself. Healing is about mending and making you whole and complete again. Emotional hurts feel like something was taken from you. That something is your peace and joy. Now what remains are wounds.

I asked some people this question: "How important is emotional healing?"

Person 1: "I haven't given it much thought."
I asked, "Do you have emotional wounds?"
He replied, "Yes, but I just live my life the best way I can."
I asked, "Do you think these wounds affect your life?"
He replied, "Oh I know they do, but I do not know what to do about this. No one has ever cared to ask this question. No one has asked me about my emotional health."
I replied, "Well buy this book that I am writing." We both laughed. I began talking to him, and now he is on the journey to healing.

Person 2: "This is crazy because I have been thinking about this. I feel like if I can get past all the damage that I have in me, I can soar. There is so much that I want to do in my life, but my pain is holding me back." Guess what? This person is now on the journey to healing.

Person 3: "It is not important. I know that I have emotional hurts, but this is a part of life. It's called being human." This person was completely closed to healing.

Person 4: It is so important. I am in my process of healing now and there is nothing like it.

Through the stories and questions that I have asked for this book, people are already on the journey to healing. This is amazing. I am tired of us walking around emotionally and mentally damaged. I want us healed and set from the bondage of pain.
I want to give some scriptures that you can mediate on as we are on this journey.

Healing scriptures:
Jeremiah 17:14 NIV
"Heal me, Lord, and I will be healed; save me and I will be saved, for you are the one I praise."

Jeremiah 17:14 NLT
"O Lord, if you heal me, I will be truly healed; if you save me, I will be truly saved. My praises are for you alone!"

Isaiah 53:4-5 NIV
"Surely, he took up our pain and bore our suffering, yet we considered him punished by God, stricken by him, and afflicted. But he was pierced for our transgressions, he was crushed for our iniquities; the

punishment that brought us peace was on him, and by his wounds we are healed."

Isaiah 53:4-5 AMP
"But [in fact] He has borne our griefs, And He has carried our sorrows and pains; Yet we [ignorantly] assumed that He was stricken, Struck down by God and degraded and humiliated [by Him]. But He was wounded for our transgressions, He was crushed for our wickedness [our sin, our injustice, our wrongdoing]; The punishment [required] for our well-being fell on Him, And by His stripes (wounds) we are healed."

Jeremiah 33:6 NIV
"Nevertheless, I will bring health and healing to it; I will heal my people and will let them enjoy abundant peace and security."

3 John 1:2 NIV
"Dear friend, I pray that you may enjoy good health and that all may go well with you, even as your soul is getting along well."

3 John 1:2 AMP
"Beloved, I pray that in every way you may succeed and prosper and be in good health [physically], just as [I know] your soul prospers [spiritually]."

Philippians 4:19 NIV
"And my God will meet all your needs according to the riches of his glory in Christ Jesus."

Proverbs 4: 20-22 NIV
"My son, pay attention to what I say; turn your ear to my words. Do not let them out of your sight, keep them within your heart; for they are life to those who find them and health to one's whole body."

Proverbs 17:22 NIV
"A cheerful heart is good medicine, but a crushed spirit dries up the bones."

Isaiah 33:2 NIV
"LORD, be gracious to us; we long for you. Be our strength every morning, our salvation in time of distress."

James 5:16 NIV
"Therefore, confess your sins to each other and pray for each other so that you may be healed. The prayer of a righteous person is powerful and effective."

1 Peter 2:24 NIV
"He himself bore our sins" in his body on the cross, so that we might die to sins and live for righteousness; "by his wounds you have been healed."

John 14:27 NIV
"Peace I leave with you; my peace I give you. I do not give to you as the world gives. Do not let your hearts be troubled and do not be afraid."

Matthew 11:28-30 NIV
"Come to me, all you who are weary and burdened, and I will give you rest. Take my yoke upon you and learn from me, for I am gentle and humble in

heart, and you will find rest for your souls. For my yoke is easy and my burden is light."

Isaiah 40:29 NIV
"He gives strength to the weary and increases the power of the weak."

Psalms 107:19-21 NIV
"Then they cried to the LORD in their trouble, and he saved them from their distress. He sent out his word and healed them; he rescued them from the grave. Let them give thanks to the LORD for his unfailing love and his wonderful deeds for mankind."

Psalms 30:2 NIV
"LORD my God, I called to you for help, and you healed me."

Many of these Scriptures are promises from the Old Testament regarding Israel, but those promises still stand today. Thank God He is the same yesterday, today, and forevermore (See: Hebrews 13:8). His promises still stand. We can be healed in any way we need. Pursue healing today!

We can do this! We can be made whole. We can be healed. We must pursue our healing relentlessly and without fear. God has not given us the spirit of fear by power, love, and a sound mind. (See: 2 Timothy 1:7). Fear is a liar. We sometimes fear what we don't understand, and we also fear change. Being comfortable is a friend to pain. Pray, read, and mediate on His word. It is our guaranteed way to healing.

Questions for Reflections:

1. Do you believe God is the Healer and wants to heal you?

2. In what ways, if any, has your pain attached more pain?

3. What person can you identify with out of the four mentioned?

4. What definition of healing speaks to you the most?

5. Are you committed to read, meditate, and pray these scriptures on you for however long it takes?

Prayer:
  Father, we thank You for being our God; the One who heals and binds up our wounds. We thank You for thinking enough about our healing to send Jesus to die for us to be whole and complete. We pray complete and total healing to our bodies, emotions, and mind in the Name of Jesus. We pray that every area of our life will line up with Your Word. Thank for Your strength and Your unfailing love. Help us to not let our hearts be troubled and send Your spirit to comfort us, O God.

Father we lay down our burdens and pick up Your yoke, for Your yoke is easy and Your burdens are light. We declare that by Your strips we are healed. In the incomparable Name of Jesus. Amen.

Chapter 7- True Freedom

John 8:36 AMP
"So, if the Son makes you free, then you are unquestionably free."

I know we have the wrong concept of freedom and what that truly means, especially as it refers to being a believer. We view freedom as a license to do whatever we want when we want. This is a misconception of freedom. When you are free it doesn't mean that you are in the absence of rules, regulations, guidelines, and expectations.

What, then, is freedom?

Greek: *eleutheria*, freedom, liberty, especially a state of freedom from slavery.

Freedom: the condition of being free; the power to act or speak or think without externally imposed restraints. 21

Freedom: The state of not being subject to or affected by (something undesirable). 22

True freedom in Christ is not being a slave to pain, hurt, sin, disappointment, loss, or any such thing. When you are full of pain you are affected by many things such as the person, the situation, the offense, and more. When you hold onto things, you give up your right to be free. You allow whatever it is to take up residency in your soul. It takes more energy to hold on to pain than to let it go. When I was in the place of hurt, pain, and unforgiveness, I found that I was always tired. It was emotionally and mentally draining. You may not feel like the person or situation deserves your forgiveness. I validate those feelings. However, you deserve to be free.

Make a Decision

My friend shared this story.

I was always the kid who had a major temper. I would ruin everyone's fun because I would take things so seriously all the time. Nothing was a good time when I was around, and if it was, I made sure it wasn't after I was done. I grew up with this. I thought this made me tough. I had the attitude that no one could mess with me. I grew up being a womanizer, cheater, and a liar. I inflicted hurt on whoever, whenever I felt like it. I was beaten as a child, and my father was the same way. So why not? Also, I wanted to make sure no one would ever hurt me like he did. I didn't realize that I was hurting and that's why I caused pain. I thought I was free to make my own choices and do my thing. However, inside I was bound to fear, hurt, pain, and an image that I had to uphold. I started realizing that I needed help when what I thought I had control over had control over me. I started causing hurt and devastation on autopilot. I was trapped inside of myself when this was happening. Through the ministry of my friend, I was delivered and set free. He was the only one that wasn't scared of me because he had the Holy Spirit on the inside of Him.

I am familiar with this story because I was the one ministering to this man. It is an amazing story of healing and restoration. What is written here cannot do this story justice on how intense this experience was. But he is now a free man. Free from pain, hurt, disappointment, and devastation. I didn't set him free, but Jesus did, and who the Son sets free is free indeed.

Scriptures on freedom for you to meditate, read and pray.

Galatians 5:1 AMP
"It was for this freedom that Christ set us free [completely liberating us]; therefore, keep standing firm and do not be subject again to a yoke of slavery [which you once removed]."

1 Peter 2:16 AMP
"Live as free people, but do not use your freedom as a cover or pretext for evil, but [use it and live] as bondservants of God."

Galatians 5:13 AMP
"For you, my brothers, were called to freedom; only do not let your freedom become an opportunity for the sinful nature (worldliness, selfishness), but through love serve and seek the best for one another."

Isaiah 61:1 AMP
The Spirit of the Lord God is upon me, Because the Lord has anointed and commissioned me to bring good news to the humble and afflicted; He has sent me to bind up [the wounds of] the brokenhearted, to proclaim release [from confinement and condemnation] to the [physical and spiritual] captives and freedom to prisoners,

Romans 8:1 AMP

Therefore, there is now no condemnation [no guilty verdict, no punishment] for those who are in Christ Jesus [who believe in Him as personal Lord and Savior].

"May we think of freedom, not as the right to do as we please, but as the opportunity to do what is right." - Peter Marshall

Freedom should always be used for the right things in life. Freedom is not a means to be out of control. The Scripture says we should not use our freedom to continue to sin. We also should not use our freedom to stay in a broken, and hurting place. Freedom is releasing yourself from bondage of any kind. If you are sinning, you are bound and a slave to sin. If you are hurting, you are bound to hurt. Through Jesus there is freedom from all of that. We can be free.

Keys to Freedom:

1. Acknowledge that you are bound. Identify what you are bound to.

2. Realize that it is not in your strength or power to fix it.

3. Ask Jesus to set you free. It belongs to you through the death and resurrection of Jesus Christ.

4. Live in that freedom. Make a choice every day so that you will walk in freedom.

Questions for Reflections:

1. How would you define freedom?

2. What does it mean to be unquestionably free?

3. Are you bound to something? If so, what?

4. Have you made excuses for your pain because of what has happened to you?

5. Are you ready to be unquestionably free?

Prayer:

      Father, we thank You for the freedom that You have set before us. Lord help us to make the choice to live in freedom as you intended. We pray that you break everything in us that makes us a slave. Whether it be hurt, pain, anxiety, sin, or any such thing. We want to walk in freedom every day. We pray that You would empower us by Your Holy Spirit. In Jesus Name, Amen.

Word of God

The Lord told me a great revival would come for the church. This revival would involve the healing and strengthening of the inner man as it says in
Ephesians 3:16 AMP
May He grant you out of the riches of His glory, to be strengthened and spiritually energized with power through His Spirit in your inner self, [indwelling your innermost being and personality].

Pain and hurt has caused My Body to stay stagnant in many ways. Many churches are spending most of their talks bandaging wounds instead of furthering My Gospel. I will cause healing, and restoration shall come. As people repent and turn back to Me, I will cause a time of refreshing (See: Acts 3:20.) I will send you to different churches and regions to bring healing to broken hearts. You will cause My people to let my fire burn through them once again. You will bring healing to eyes that have been blinded spiritually through hurt, pain, and sin. I want My people healed and whole. I am coming back again soon; many will not make it because pain has caused them to harden their hearts, even towards Me. You and many others shall bring a great awakening once again to My Body. I will do this through the power of My Holy Spirit.

Journey Into Healing: Take Time To Heal

Abraham JT Harris, BBS

Study Questions

I have added a study section to further help you on your journey to healing. As one who has been through this process, these topics and verses have helped me. You will find that these thought-provoking questions will help you self- reflect and self-correct. I wanted to help you continue your journey by giving you such tools.

Study One: New Creation
2 Corinthians 5:17 NJKV
"Therefore, if anyone is in Christ, he is a new creation; old things have passed away; behold, all things have become new."

2 Corinthians 5:17 AMP
"Therefore, if anyone is in Christ [that is, grafted in, joined to Him by faith in Him as Savior], he is a new creature [reborn and renewed by the Holy Spirit]; the old things [the previous moral and spiritual condition] have passed away. Behold, new things have come [because spiritual awakening brings a new life]."

We should no longer be the same when we have asked the Lord Jesus Christ in our hearts. Our minds should change towards our old lives.

Warming- Up

1. How do you experience this newness in Christ?

2. What does it mean to be "In Christ?"

Digging in
Read: Luke 5: 33-39

3. Jesus used a parable about New Wine in Old Wine skins. What was he trying to convey to the listeners?

4. What does wine signify?

5. What do you believe is the overall meaning of this parable?

Study Two: Hope
Romans 5:5 NKJV

"Now hope does not disappoint, because the love of God has been poured out in our hearts by the Holy Spirit who was given to us."

Hope: 1680 *elpís* (from *elpō*, "to anticipate, welcome") – properly, expectation of what is sure (certain); hope.

Warming- up

1. Why do you think Paul writes, "hope does not disappoint?"

2. What is the love of God? How have you experience the love of God?

Digging In
Read: Judges 6

3. What was Gideon's response when he was told he was chosen by God?

4. How many signs did Gideon ask for?

5. What gave Gideon hope? What was the outcome?

Study Three: Healing
Acts 10: 36-38 NKJV

"The word which God sent to the children of Israel, preaching peace through Jesus Christ— He is Lord of all— that word you know, which was proclaimed throughout all Judea, and began from Galilee after the baptism which John preached: how God anointed Jesus of Nazareth with the Holy Spirit and with power, who went about doing good and healing all who were oppressed by the devil, for God was with Him."

Warming- Up

1. Does it give you comfort to know that Jesus came to heal?

2. What does it mean to be oppressed?

Digging In:
Read: Mark 5:25–34

3. What do you believe was driving this woman to do this?

4. Have you considered that one touch from Jesus will heal you?

5. What gave this woman the courage to get to Jesus?

Study Four: Trust
Proverbs 3:5-6 NKJV

"Trust in the LORD with all your heart, and lean not on your own understanding; In all your ways acknowledge Him, And He shall direct your paths."

Truth: 225. *alétheia* truth, but not merely truth as spoken; truth of idea, reality, sincerity, truth in the moral sphere, divine truth revealed to man, straightforwardness.

Warming Up

1. What do the words "All of your heart" mean to you?

2. What does it mean to lean not on your own understanding?

Digging In
Read: Genesis 22: 1-19

3. What was God asking Abraham to do?

4. What was Abraham's response to God's request?

5. God provided for Abraham. What does this story teach you about trust in God?

Study Five: Faith
Hebrews 11:1 ESV
"Now faith is the assurance of things hoped for, the conviction of things not seen."
Matthew 21:22 ESV
"And whatever you ask in prayer, you will receive, if you have faith."

Faith: *PISTIS* means faith, belief, firm persuasion, assurance, firm conviction, faithfulness.

Warming Up
1. Define faith in your words.

2. Why is faith necessary when praying?

Digging in
Read: Daniel 3
3. Why do you think the Hebrews would not obey the King?

4. Daniel 3:17-18 NJKV
"If that is the case, our God whom we serve is able to deliver us from the burning fiery furnace, and He will deliver us from your hand, O king. But if not, let it be known to you, O king, that we do not serve your gods, nor will we worship the gold image which you have set up."

5. What does this story teach you about faith in God?

Study 6: What You Speak Matters
Proverbs 18:21 NJKV
"Death and life are in the power of the tongue, and those who love it will eat its fruit."

Warming Up
1. What does this verse mean to you?

1 Peter 3:10 NKJV
"He who would love life and see good days, let him refrain his tongue from evil, and his lips from speaking deceit."

2. What does refrain mean?

3. What does the love of life and good days have to do with the tongue?

Digging In
Colossians 4:6 NKJV
"Let your speech always be with grace, seasoned with salt, that you may know how you ought to answer each one."

4. Why is it important that our speech be "seasoned with salt?"

Ephesians 4:29 NKJV
"Let no corrupt word proceed out of your mouth, but what is good for necessary edification, that it may impart grace to the hearers."

5. What is a corrupt word?

Study Seven: Strength
Psalms 46:1 NKJV
God is our refuge and strength, A very present help in trouble.

Dunamis (POWER): (miraculous) power, might, strength. Physical power, force, might, ability, efficacy, energy, meaning (b) *plur*: powerful deeds, deeds showing (physical) power, marvelous works.

Warming Up
1. In what ways do you think God is our strength?

2. What does present help mean?

Digging in
Read: Judges 13-16
3. What did God give Samson?

Read: Judges 13:25; 14:6, 19; 15:14
4. Who was the source of Samson's supernatural strength?

5. What did God require of Samson?

Study Eight: Integrity
Proverbs 15:32-33 NKJV
"He who disdains instruction despises his own soul, but he who heeds rebuke gets understanding. The fear of the Lord is the instruction of wisdom, and before honor is humility."

Warming Up

1. Why is instruction important to your soul?

2. God loves humility. Why do you think this is the case?

Digging In
Proverbs 25:27-28 NKJV
It is not good to eat much honey; So to seek one's own glory is not glory. Whoever has no rule over his own spirit is like a city broken down, without walls.

3. Why did the writer refer to a city broken down? What does this mean?

Psalm 84:11 NKJV
For the Lord God is a sun and shield; The LORD will give grace and glory; No good thing will He withhold from those who walk uprightly.

4. What is grace?

5. What does it mean to "walk uprightly"?

Study Nine: Power
2 Corinthians 4:7-10 NKJV

"But we have this treasure in earthen vessels, that the excellence of the power may be of God and not of us. We are hard-pressed on every side, yet not crushed; we are perplexed, but not in despair; persecuted, but not forsaken; struck down, but not destroyed— always carrying about in the body the dying of the Lord Jesus, that the life of Jesus also may be manifested in our body."

Warming Up

1. What is this treasure?

2 Corinthians 12:7-10 NRSV

"Even considering the exceptional character of the revelations. Therefore, to keep me from being too elated, a thorn was given me in the flesh, a messenger of Satan to torment me, to keep me from being too elated. Three times I appealed to the Lord about this, that it would leave me, but he said to me, "My grace is sufficient for you, for power is made perfect in weakness." So, I will boast all the more gladly of my weaknesses, so that the power of Christ may dwell in me. Therefore, I am content with weaknesses, insults, hardships, persecutions, and calamities for the sake of Christ; for whenever I am weak, then I am strong."

2. What does sufficient mean?

3. What is the power of Christ?

Digging In
James 1:21 NRSV
"Therefore rid yourselves of all sordidness and rank growth of wickedness, and welcome with meekness the implanted word that has the power to save your souls."

4. What does it mean to rid yourself?

5. What is the implanted word?

Study Ten: Believe
Mark 9:23 NKJV
Jesus said to him, "If you can believe, all things are possible to him who believes."

Warming Up
1. Can you ever recall a time where you believed something so strongly that it came to pass?

2. What does the word "possible" mean?

Digging in
Read: Luke 17: 11-19
3. What is a Leper?

4. What did Jesus tell them to do? Why was it important that they did so?

5. Why did Jesus say, "Your Faith has made you well?"

Journey Into Healing: Take Time To Heal

Notes:

Chapter 1

1. "Adapt: Definition of Adapt by Lexico." Lexico Dictionaries | English, Lexico Dictionaries, www.lexico.com/en/definition/adapt.
2. "Move: Definition of Move by Lexico." Lexico Dictionaries | English, Lexico Dictionaries, www.lexico.com/en/definition/move.
3. "Forward." Dictionary.com, Dictionary.com, www.dictionary.com/browse/forward.
4. Strong's Greek: 1922. Ἐπίγνωσις (Epignósis) -- Recognition, Knowledge, biblehub.com/greek/1922.htm.
5. "Genesis 1:1 (KJV)." Blue Letter Bible, www.blueletterbible.org/lang/lexicon/lexicon.cfm?t=kjv&strongs=h3045.

Chapter 2

6. "Does Time Heal All Wounds? The Center for Grief Recovery and Therapeutic Services." Center for Grief Recovery and Therapeutic Services, 19 Mar. 2018, griefcounselor.org/does-time-heal-all-wounds.
7. "Time: Definition of Time by Lexico." Lexico Dictionaries | English, Lexico Dictionaries, www.lexico.com/en/definition/time.

Chapter 3

8. "Aphesis Meaning in Bible - New Testament Greek Lexicon - New American Standard." Bible Study Tools, www.biblestudytools.com/lexicons/greek/nas/aphesis.html.
9. "Forgiving." Merriam-Webster, Merriam-Webster, www.merriam-webster.com/dictionary/forgiving.
10. Be fruitful, Comments. "12 Inspirational Rick Warren Quotes On Forgiveness." IPost, ipost.christianpost.com/post/12-inspirational-rick-warren-quotes-on-forgiveness.
11. "We Win by Tenderness. We Conquer by Forgiveness. at QuoteTab." QuoteTab, www.quotetab.com/quote/by-frederick-william-robertson/we-win-by-tenderness-we-conquer-by-forgiveness?source=conquer.
12. "Forgiving the Inexcusable." Right from The Heart Ministries, rightfromtheheart.org/devotions/forgiving-the-inexcusable/.
13. Guillemets, Terri. Forgiveness Quotes & Sayings (Forgiving, I Forgive You, Forgive & Forget, Accepting Apologies, Etc), www.quotegarden.com/forgiveness.html.

Chapter 4

14. "Experience." Merriam-Webster, Merriam-Webster, www.merriam-webster.com/dictionary/experience.
15. "Express." Merriam-Webster, Merriam-Webster, www.merriam-webster.com/dictionary/express.
16. "Exit." Merriam-Webster, Merriam-Webster, www.merriam-webster.com/dictionary/exit.
17. Strong's Greek: 341. Ἀνακαινόω (Anakainoó) -- 2 Occurrences, biblehub.com/greek/strongs_341.htm.

Chapter 5

18. Bible Topics: Brokenness, deeptruths.com/bible-topics/brokenness.html.
19. "KJV Dictionary Definition: Contrite." AV1611.Com, av1611.com/kjbp/kjv-dictionary/contrite.html.

Chapter 6

20. Bible, Online. "Define HEAL: Definition for Word HEAL Vine's Greek New Testament Dictionary HEAL." Define HEAL | Definition for Word HEAL Vine's Greek New Testament Dictionary HEAL,

gospelhall.org/bible/bible.php?search=HEAL&dict=vine&lang=english.
21. "Heal." Merriam-Webster, Merriam-Webster, www.merriam-webster.com/dictionary/heal.
22. "HEALING | Definition in the Cambridge English Dictionary." Google, Google, www.google.com/amp/s/dictionary.cambridge.org/us/amp/english/healing.
23. "Healing." Dictionary.com, Dictionary.com, www.dictionary.com/browse/healing.
24. Twooney, Madeline. "What Does It Mean That God Is Jehovah-Rapha?" Christianity.com, Salem Web Network, 10 July 2019, www.christianity.com/wiki/god/what-does-it-mean-that-god-is-jehovah-rapha.html.

Chapter 7

25. Strong's Greek: 1657. Ἐλευθερία (Eleutheria) -- Liberty, Freedom, biblehub.com/greek/1657.htm.
26. "Freedom - Dictionary Definition." Vocabulary.com, www.vocabulary.com/dictionary/freedom.
27. "Freedom: Definition of Freedom by Lexico." Lexico Dictionaries | English, Lexico Dictionaries, www.lexico.com/en/definition/freedom.
28. "May We Think of Freedom Not as the Right to Do as We Please, but as the Opportunity to Do What Is Right." Passiton.com,

www.passiton.com/inspirational-quotes/7776-may-we-think-of-freedom-not-as-the-right-to-do.

29. Strong's Greek: 1680. Ἐλπίς (Elpis) -- Expectation, Hope, biblehub.com/greek/1680.htm.
30. "Hebrew Roots/The Original Foundation/Faith." Hebrew Roots/The Original Foundation/Faith - Wikibooks, Open Books for an Open World, en.wikibooks.org/wiki/Hebrew_Roots/The_original_foundation/Faith.
31. Strong's Greek: 225. Ἀλήθεια (Alétheia) -- Truth, biblehub.com/greek/225.htm.
32. Bible, Online. "Define BELIEVE: Definition for Word BELIEVE Vine's Greek New Testament Dictionary BELIEVE." Define BELIEVE | Definition for Word BELIEVE Vine's Greek New Testament Dictionary BELIEVE, gospelhall.org/bible/bible.php?search=BELIEVE&dict=vine&lang=english.
33. Greek: 1411. Δύναμις (Dunamis) -- (Miraculous) Power, Might, Strength, biblehub.com/greek/1411.htm.

Journey Into Healing: Take Time To Heal